The Library of Author Biographies™

James Lincoln Collier

The Library of Author Biographies™

JAMES LINCOLN COLLIER

Liz Sonneborn

The Rosen Publishing Group, Inc., New York

Published in 2006 by The Rosen Publishing Group, Inc.
29 East 21st Street, New York, NY 10010

Library of Congress Cataloging-in-Publication Data

Sonneborn, Liz.
James Lincoln Collier / by Liz Sonneborn.— 1st ed.
    p. cm.—(The library of author biographies)
Includes bibliographical references and index.
ISBN 1-4042-0461-X (lib. bdg.)
ISBN 1-4042-0649-3 (pbk. bdg.)
1. Collier, James Lincoln, 1928– 2. Authors, American—20th century—Biography. 3. Young adult fiction—Authorship.
4. Historical fiction—Authorship. I. Title. II. Series.
PS3553.O4746345Z88 2006
813'.54—dc22

                                                      2004025552

Manufactured in the United States of America

Excerpt from THE JAZZ KID by James Lincoln Collier, © 1997. Reprinted by permission of Henry Holt and Company, LLC.
From CONTEMPORARY AUTHORS ONLINE, by Gale Group © 2004, Gale Group. Reprinted by permission of the Gale Group.
100 Most Popular Children's Authors: Biographical Sketches and Bibliographies. Copyright © (1999) by Libraries Unlimited. Reproduced with permission of Greenwood Publishing Group, Inc., Westport, CT.
Reprinted by permission from THE BOOK REPORT, Volume 15, Issue 2, Copyright © 1996 by Linworth Publishing, Inc.
From WHO IS CARRIE? by James Lincoln Collier and Christopher Collier, copyright © 1984 by James Lincoln Collier and Christopher Collier. Cover painting by Gordon Crabb. Used by permission of Dell Publishing, a division of Random House Inc.
From WAR COMES TO WILLY FREEMAN by James Lincoln Collier and Christopher Collier, copyright © 1983 by James Lincoln Collier and Christopher Collier. Used by permission of Dell Publishing, a division of Random House Inc.
Reprinted with the permission of Simon & Schuster Books for Young Readers, an imprint of Simon & Schuster Children's Publishing Division from THE WINTER HERO by James Lincoln Collier and Christopher Collier. Copyright © 1978 James Lincoln Collier and Christopher Collier.
Reprinted with the permission of Simon & Schuster Books for Young Readers, an imprint of Simon & Schuster Children's Publishing Division from THE BLOODY COUNTRY by James Lincoln Collier and Christopher Collier. Copyright © 1976 James Lincoln Collier and Christopher Collier.
Reprinted with the permission of Simon & Schuster Books for Young Readers, an imprint of Simon & Schuster Children's Publishing Division from MY BROTHER SAM IS DEAD by James Lincoln Collier and Christopher Collier. Copyright © 1974 James Lincoln Collier and Christopher Collier.
From JUMP SHIP TO FREEDOM by James Lincoln Collier and Christopher Collier, copyright © 1981 by James Lincoln Collier and Christopher Collier. Used by permission of Dell Publishing, a division of Random House Inc.
From Fifth Book of Juniors Authors, Copyright (1983), edited by Sally Holmes Holtze. Reprinted with permission of The H.W. Wilson Company.
The Horn Book Magazine, April 1976. Reprinted by permission of The Horn Book, Inc., Boston, MA, www.hbook.com.
From AUTHORS AND ARTISTS FOR YOUNG ADULTS, 13, by Gale Group, © 1994, Gale Group. Reprinted by permission of the Gale Group.
Banned in the U.S.A.: A Reference Guide to Book Censorship in Schools and Public Libraries, Rev. ed., by Foerstel, Herbert N., Copyright © 2002 by Greenwood Press. Reproduced with permission of Greenwood Publishing Group, Inc., Westport, CT.

Table of Contents

Introduction:
Fact and Fiction

Some writers become masters of a single subject. Others focus on writing for a particular audience. Still others devote all their time and energy to a specific genre, concentrating on, say, mysteries or horror stories.

And then there is James Lincoln Collier.

Collier has had an amazing career. For five decades, he has been a successful writer. Early on, Collier wrote for magazines, producing hundreds of articles. But since the 1970s, he has concentrated on writing books. He now has about 100 to his credit.

The sheer volume of work Collier has produced is startling. But even more impressive is his range as a writer. He has written on many different subjects, for both adults and children.

Collier is equally adept at writing nonfiction and fiction. Works of nonfiction are based on factual research, while works of fiction are stories that come from a writer's imagination.

Given Collier's skill with both facts and fiction, it is not surprising he is best known for writing a type of book that combines the two—the historical novel. Historical novels tell stories that blend the real and the imagined. Set sometime in the past, they include events that actually happened and people who actually lived. But these real elements are placed in stories invented in the author's mind.

As a testament to his mastery of the historical novel, Collier was awarded the Phoenix Award in 1994 for *My Brother Sam Is Dead*, which was published twenty years earlier in 1974. Written with his younger brother, Christopher, this young adult novel about the American Revolution was honored for standing the test of time.

This classic also displays two of Collier's great strengths as a writer. Through his extensive reading and research, he is able to explore just about any subject, learning its every aspect so well that he can explain it to audiences of all ages. And through his gift for storytelling, he is able to create fresh and exciting narratives, impressing hundreds of critics, delighting thousands of readers, and creating a legion of fans for his work.

1 A Writer's Life

James Lincoln Collier was born in New York City on June 27, 1928. The Collier family had long lived to the north in New England. But his parents had chosen to settle in New York, attracted by the city's artistic and intellectual circles. According to Collier, his view of the world comes from a combination of New England traditions and New York City values: "[My family] grew up in this mix of cultures, one side of which valued hard work, human decency and a respect for the privacy of others; the other of which valued high-minded intellectuality, adherence to principle and a concern for the truth."[1]

When he was still a boy, his family moved again, this time to Wilton, a small town in

Connecticut. Life in this rural setting was completely different from life in the big city. His younger brother, Christopher (nicknamed Kit), later recalled that their home was surrounded by farms. He remembered fondly the quiet pleasures of the town, where he and James played outside without ever hearing the noise of passing cars.

While growing up, the Collier boys were more than brothers. They were best friends. The Colliers spent much of their time together, though they did occasionally fight. Christopher claims that his older brother usually ended up getting the best of him. As he explains, "When we were kids, he always won every argument. He might not agree with that, but that's how it seemed to me."[2]

Some of James's favorite childhood memories are of visits to the home of his uncle, writer William Slater Brown. Brown was friends with several famous American authors, including Hart Crane, John Dos Passos, and Malcolm Cowley. As Collier notes, "For a period of time in the twenties and thirties, this house was a hangout for some very interesting people."[3] Collier now owns the house, where he often spends weekends. Its literary heritage still excites him. He recently explained during an interview, "Hart Crane wrote portions of [the poem] 'The Bridge' in my bedroom!"[4]

After high school, James Lincoln Collier attended Hamilton College in Clinton, New York. Immediately after graduation, he was drafted into the U.S. Army and served a brief stint in the infantry during the Korean War (1951–1952). When Collier was discharged in 1951, he knew exactly what he would do with the rest of his life— he would be a writer.

Beginnings

Collier's decision was hardly a surprise. His family is full of writers. His father wrote adventure stories and biographies for children. An uncle, an aunt, and several cousins were professional writers as well. In fact, the Collier family's interest in writing stretched over many generations, all the way back to colonial times. Collier is distantly related to Anne Bradstreet, one of America's first poets.

Growing up among writers and around writing, Collier had no doubt that he could make his way in his chosen profession. As he explains, "It never occurred to me that I couldn't write; it was what people did, and it has been what I have done since I became an adult."[5] But Collier also had no illusions about how difficult it is to make money as a writer, as his father's career had taught him. According to Collier, his father "wrote western fiction until the Depression came along. Then he couldn't earn a living at it any more. He became a tree surgeon."[6]

To pursue his career, Collier moved back to New York City, settling in the neighborhood of Greenwich Village. In the 1950s, Greenwich Village was filled with inexpensive apartments that drew aspiring artists and writers. The neighborhood attracted Collier for another reason, too. A talented trombonist, he found part-time work playing at the many jazz clubs along the Village's narrow streets.

Collier married his first wife, Carol Burrows, in 1952. They soon started a family, which included two sons, Geoffrey and Andrew. (Collier and Burrows were later divorced; in 1983, Collier married his second wife, Ida Karen Potash.) To support his family, Collier took a day job as a magazine editor. On weekends and evenings, he spent any moments of spare time writing.

In 1958, he decided to plunge into writing full-time. He quit his magazine job and became a freelance writer. To make ends meet, he wrote at a furious pace, producing for publication as many as 600,000 words (about 2,500 typewritten pages) a year. He wrote hundreds of articles for all types of magazines, from *Reader's Digest* to *TV Guide*.

Making a Living

For most freelance writers, earning a decent living is a challenge. The competition is fierce, the pay is often low, and assignments are sometimes hard to come by. Also, to pay their bills, freelancers have to write what sells. Often, that means they have to put their more personal projects aside.

Collier is candid about his own struggles early in his career. It was hard to earn enough money to take care of his wife and children. But he also sees an upside to having to concentrate on writing sellable material. He explains, "The economic goad was critically important in teaching me that what I wrote had first of all to be interesting to real people."[7]

In Collier's eyes, a professional writer cannot wait for inspiration. He acknowledges that some days he has forced himself to sit down and write. By writing day after day, Collier not only produces a great deal of work, but he also carefully hones his craft, constantly learning new ways to approach his subjects and better ways to write about them. Collier himself feels that his best work has emerged from the lessons about writing he has taught himself over the years: "My best-liked books have always been those written not out of a fiery vision but as a professional, using sleights of hand that took me years to discover and develop."[8]

Collier attributes his willingness to work hard at his writing to his upbringing. He explains, "My forebears were New Englanders, and I was raised to an old morality that stressed hard work and the joys of accomplishment. Undoubtedly this background helped to give me the self-discipline a writer needs."[9] But as difficult as writing can be, Collier also finds it endlessly involving. He often concentrates so hard on his work that he forgets about the world around him. According to Collier, when he gets involved in his writing, he does not even know whether the sun is shining outside.

From Articles to Books

While still writing for magazines, Collier began to venture into books. In the early 1960s, he wrote two novels for adults. His agent, who negotiated his book deals, then suggested that Collier try writing for children. The agent convinced him that he could make a good living writing children's books.

Collier's first effort was *Battleground: The United States Army in World War II* (1965). *School Library Journal* praised the book. According to reviewer Robert Kinchen, "[*Battleground* is a] history of the U.S. Army in World War II with special emphasis on individual heroes and their deeds . . . In addition to his treatment of personalities, the author provides an easy-to-follow overview of the war as it affected the U.S. Army ground forces."[10]

Collier followed up *Battleground* with several more nonfiction books for children. He introduced young readers to the world of firefighters and doctors in *A Visit to the Fire House* (1967) and *Danny Goes to the Hospital* (1970). For young adults, he wrote several books about one of his favorite subjects—music. Collier also began writing novels for children. His first, *The Teddy Bear Habit* (1967), highlights Collier's flair both for comedy and for exciting adventure stories. Jerome Beatty Jr., writing in the *New York Times Book Review*, declared, "'The Teddy Bear Habit' develops into a heck of an exciting story with a combination of humor and suspense, and a lack of fake sentiment, that is refreshing to find in a children's book."[11]

With the success of *The Teddy Bear Habit*, Collier wrote more novels for young adults with contemporary settings, including *Rock Star* (1970), *It's Murder at St. Basket's* (1972), and *Rich and Famous* (1975), a sequel to *Habit*. Although he continued to write nonfiction for adults, Collier was increasingly drawn to children's literature, in part because of his admiration for young readers. He explains, "It seems to me that the best audience for fiction in the United States is young people. Unimpressed by prizes and reviews, they read what they like, and to a surprising extent they like the best."[12]

2 Collaborating

B y the early 1970s, James Lincoln Collier was an established writer, with some fifteen books to his credit. But his career took a dramatic shift when he agreed to work on a project dreamed up by his younger brother, Christopher. As Christopher Collier tells it, he had been after James for fifteen years to collaborate with him on a historical novel for teenagers. Christopher claims that James was too busy with other projects to take on the book Christopher envisioned.

Teaming Up

In interviews, James remembers the beginnings of their collaboration differently. He says he

17

was far more receptive to Christopher's proposal: "When Kit broached the idea underlying *My Brother Sam Is Dead* [the first book the Colliers wrote together], I quickly saw the possibilities in it." So did his editor, even though, as Collier later recalled, "at the time publishers believed that historical fiction for children did not sell well."[1]

Christopher, though, was determined to find an audience for the book. For many years, he had been a professor of history at the University of Bridgeport and the University of Connecticut. But his first job after graduating from college was teaching students at several Connecticut junior high schools. There, he saw firsthand how uninspiring his students found their history books. He was sure "there must be a better—more interesting and memorable—way to teach such exciting stuff as history is made of than through the dull, dull textbooks we used."[2] Collier decided "that kids would learn better and remember more if they learned history through really exciting, but true, novels."[3]

Like most professional historians, Christopher Collier was already a writer. He had written several scholarly books and many articles about his area of expertise—the history of America in the late eighteenth century, especially the Revolutionary

War era (1775–1783). One of his books, *Roger Sherman's Connecticut: Yankee Politics and the American Revolution* (1971), was nominated for the prestigious Pulitzer Prize. Although Christopher Collier was an accomplished writer of history, he had had no experience writing fiction or writing for children. Teaming up with James to write historical novels, then, seemed perfect: Christopher could oversee the historical accuracy of the book, while James could ensure it told a good story that young readers would enjoy.

Working Together

Working on *My Brother Sam Is Dead*, the Collier brothers developed a way of collaborating that they have used to produce all their novels. The book begins in Christopher's head. He thinks of an idea he wants to teach, matching it with a historic event that can be dramatized to illustrate his point. Christopher then discusses it with James, who evaluates whether he can make an exciting story out of the event. James has to consider many things. The event has to contain plenty of action, for instance. Since the protagonists of their books are adolescents, the story also has to deal with a historic event in which young people could play an active role.

If James likes Christopher's suggestion, they begin work. Even when they are busy with other projects, James maintains that if they are enthusiastic enough about an idea, they find the time to do it. The first task falls to Christopher. He researches the setting and events in the story and writes an outline. It proposes characters and offers a rough description of what will happen in the story. James then reads the outline. At this point, he often suggests changes to make sure the story is as dramatic as possible.

Once their editor approves the outline, Christopher begins his extensive research into the novel's subject. He gathers books and articles about the events to be covered and studies government records, newspapers, letters, diaries, and even gravestones from the period. He also looks for historical maps and drawings to help James visualize the setting. Together or separately, the Colliers often take trips to the places where the novel's action will take place and photograph the landscape. They also like to visit any historical museums that might help them understand the people and period they will be writing about.

After James has studied all the research materials, he sits down to write. With Christopher's blessing, James produces a complete first draft. As long as the draft is true to the historical facts, James feels free to veer from Christopher's outline in order to make the story more compelling. As Christopher sees it, James "is the one who makes the stories fun to read, interesting and exciting, sometimes funny. Most of all, . . . he gives the individuals in the books character and personality. That's really essential; nobody will like the books if they don't like the people in them."[4] James believes that drafting the entire first manuscript on his own is an essential element to his and Christopher's successful collaboration: "This is so that there is a consistency of language of feeling, of 'tone,' a hard-to-define quality that is nonetheless present in most good writing."[5]

Revising the Manuscript

When the draft is finished, James sends it to Christopher. Christopher reads it to check that everything is historically accurate. In one instance, he asked James to rework a scene in *My Brother Sam Is Dead*, in which two male characters had a conversation while washing dinner dishes. Christopher pointed out that, in eighteenth-century America, washing dishes was considered women's work. James responded by moving the characters out to the barn, where they talked while caring for farm animals. When Christopher receives the first draft, he also researches any new questions James might have. For instance, in the course of writing, James sometimes realizes he needs more information about the landscape of a particular setting.

Christopher sometimes also makes suggestions for improving the story. He might point out that a particular scene is not as interesting as it could be. Or he might question whether a character's behavior at a certain point makes sense. Although James welcomes Christopher's critique, they both understand that James is ultimately responsible for the plot and characters. They also agree that Christopher makes all calls regarding historical accuracy. In James's eyes, it is this division of labor and responsibility that allows the Colliers to work so well together:

> Collaboration, I think, is always difficult. I would not attempt it with just anyone. It is important to work with someone who can work out ground rules and stick to them, someone who thinks the way you do about most things and, above all someone with whom you can have a measure of mutual respect.[6]

After discussing the manuscript with Christopher, James writes a complete second draft.

Christopher again reads and comments on this version, and James again writes another draft to fix any problems he sees. The final manuscript then goes to the editor, who often asks for some minor changes before the manuscript is published.

Making It Accurate

One unusual feature of the Colliers' collaborations is the "How Much Is True" section that concludes their books. Here, they explain which events and characters are part of the historical record and which are purely their own inventions. They also explain how gaps in what historians know have guided some of their creative decisions. For example, as a rule, their characters use modern speech. As the Colliers explain, using familiar speech patterns makes the dialogue easier for young readers to understand. It is also necessary since historians of today do not really know how people spoke in earlier times.

Both Christopher and James pride themselves in their books' historical accuracy. According to Christopher, "My books for teen-agers are just as thoroughly researched as are my scholarly works. If we say it snowed three inches on January 4, 1787, in Springfield, Massachusetts, then you can be sure that it really did."[7] The "How Much Is True" section, however, allows them to head off questions readers might have about some seemingly improbable scenes. One example occurs in a dramatic scene in the Colliers' 1981 novel *Jump Ship to Freedom*. In the book, during a storm at sea, a pair of seamen are swept off the deck and into the water by a giant wave. Then, a moment later, another wave carries one of the men back on the ship to safety. Christopher acknowledges that this episode might seem unreal, but a similar event actually happened during the sea voyage of an eighteenth-century merchant ship. As Christopher explains:

> It is amazing that some of the episodes in our books that are true are the most unbelievable . . . Some of the things we make up are easy to believe, but they never happened at all. Truth is often more interesting than fiction. A combination of both is what makes our books historical fiction.[8]

Aiding the reader in separating fact from fiction also helps Christopher achieve another mission— making the books effective as teaching tools. In their collaborations, one of his goals is to increase students' curiosity about history and to get them to start asking questions. James shares his brother's desire to show young people just how exciting history can be. But James also hopes his books affect the minds and hearts of his readers in an even greater way. "My approach to writing is different than Kit's," James explains. "When I write I try deliberately to catch readers up in my story, to make them feel things, and in the end, if I am very lucky, to change their internal landscape a little by showing them a new way of looking at the world."[9]

3 Brother Sam and Other "Heroes"

In 1974, *My Brother Sam Is Dead*—the first historical novel by the Collier brothers—was published. It was greeted by nearly universal critical acclaim. Many called it an instant classic. For instance, a reviewer for the *Horn Book Magazine*, declared, "This stirring and authoritative novel earns a place beside our best historical fiction."[1] The book was also praised by the Association for Library Service to Children. Each year, this organization gives the John Newbery Medal to the author who has made the greatest contribution to American literature for children. *My Brother Sam Is Dead* did not win the medal, but it received the next best award. It was named a Newbery Honor Book for 1975.

In her review for *Washington Post Book World*, Joyce Alpern wrote, "*My Brother Sam* is obviously, at times very unsubtly, an antiwar novel."[2] Its antiwar stance probably contributed much to *My Brother Sam*'s initial success. When it was written, the United States was involved in the Vietnam War (1954–1975), a war that many Americans opposed. Although *My Brother Sam* was set long ago during the American Revolution, its commentary on the destructiveness of war seemed particularly important during the Vietnam War era. Since then, however, *My Brother Sam* has remained popular. Even in times of peace, readers have been drawn to its story of an average family caught up in a bloody conflict.

War and the Meekers

My Brother Sam focuses on the Meeker family. The Meekers operate a tavern in the town of Redding in the colony of Connecticut. They have two sons: Tim, the novel's thirteen-year-old narrator, and Sam, Tim's older brother. The difficulties facing the Meekers are spelled out in the book's first scene. Tim describes a fight between Sam and his father, Life (short for Eliphalets). Sam had run away to join the patriot army. The patriots were Americans determined to fight for their independence from the control of their mother country, England. Life disapproves of Sam's actions and resents his disobedience. In this way, early in the book, the Colliers establish a parallel between the colonies rebelling against the English king and Sam rebelling against an authority even closer to home, his father.

The Colliers present the American Revolution as not just a conflict that pitted patriots against British soldiers. They also depict it as a civil war, in which Americans fought Americans. About 20 percent of Americans were confirmed Loyalists. Loyal to the English government, they were willing to fight American patriots on England's behalf. The Colliers chose Redding as the setting of *My Brother Sam* because it had particularly strong Loyalist ties. The people of Redding were almost equally divided between patriots and Loyalists.

Early in the novel, Sam presents many reasons for supporting the patriot cause. He claims that the king, far away in England, has no right to tax or make laws for the colonists. Life outright dismisses the argument, asking, "Is it worth war to save a few pence in taxes?"[3] Sam then insists that independence is a principle worth fighting and dying for. His father, though, is skeptical: "Principle, Sam? You may know principle, Sam, but I know war. Have you ever seen a dear friend lying in the grass with the top of his skull off and his brains sliding out like wet oats?"[4] Life opposes the patriots, but he is less a Loyalist than a pacifist—someone who believes all wars are wrong.

Tim's Struggle

Sam and Life's debate provides a backdrop to the main focus of the novel: the way the war affects Tim's view of the world and his view of himself. At first, Tim sees the revolution as an adventure and envies Sam's part in it. He is eager to get into the fight on either side: "I wonder if I went for a soldier, which army would I join? The British had the best uniforms and the shiny new guns, but there was something exciting about the Patriots—being underdogs and fighting off the mighty British army."[5]

As the war intensifies, Tim's ideas about it become more complicated. For a while, Tim constantly changes his position, depending on how the fighting affects the Meekers. But as he sees more death around him, he, like his father, loses faith in both the patriots' and the Loyalists' cause: "It seemed to me that everybody was to blame, and I decided that I wasn't going to be on anybody's side any more. Neither one of them was right."[6]

Tim also comes to suspect that Sam's reasons for joining the patriots are not so noble as Sam would have others believe. He concludes that Sam just likes being a soldier—that "he was staying in the army because he wanted to."[7]

Writing about *My Brother Sam*, Christopher Collier has explained that "as soon as a people get into a war, they have lost control of events. The illogical, the inexplicable—not to mention the unjust—are an inevitable result."[8] The illogic of war is highlighted by the Colliers' use of irony in the novel. A situation is ironic when it turns out opposite to the way one would expect it to.

The two great tragedies in the novel—the deaths of Life and of Sam—are particularly ironic. Life is taken captive and dies of disease aboard an English prison ship. Although he opposed the patriots' cause, Life dies at the hands of the English soldiers. At the novel's end, Sam fights off thieves who are trying to steal the Meekers' precious cattle. Sam is mistakenly accused of stealing—an offense that carries the death penalty in the patriot army. Ironically, Sam is executed by fellow patriots.

The last chapter of *My Brother Sam* presents a final irony. The year is 1826, and Tim Meeker is sixty-four years old. He notes, "Free of British domination, the nation has prospered and I along with it."[9] But remembering the loss of his brother, father, and so many others, he still wonders whether the revolution was worth it: "I keep thinking that there might have been another way, besides war, to achieve the same end."[10]

The Bloody Country

The Colliers followed up the success of *My Brother Sam* with two more historical novels dealing with the aftermath of the American Revolution—*The Bloody Country* (1976) and *The Winter Hero* (1978). While *My Brother Sam* explores the devastation of the war itself, these later books focus on how citizens of the new United States struggled during the Confederation era, the eight-year period (1781–1789) when the country was governed under the Articles of Confederation. (In 1789, the Articles were replaced by the U.S. Constitution.) In these novels, the characters have to cope with laws made by a distant government that threaten their very way of life.

The Bloody Country takes place in the Wyoming Valley of what is now Pennsylvania. As the story begins, the family of nine-year-old Ben Buck operates a mill, a building where grain is ground into flour. Like most of their neighbors, the Bucks came to the Wyoming Valley from Connecticut in the 1770s. As Connecticut became overcrowded, these pioneers were lured west by the promise of good farmland.

But the Bucks' hope for a prosperous new life is continually threatened—most powerfully by a political dispute entirely out of their control. At the time of the American Revolution, the Wyoming Valley was claimed by two colonies, Connecticut and Pennsylvania. The valley's settlers from Pennsylvania became angry that newcomers from Connecticut were setting up farms there.

The tensions first came to a head in 1778, when Pennsylvania settlers joined with Loyalists and Native Americans in an attack on the Wyoming Valley. The encounter provides one of the most dramatic episodes in *The Bloody Country*. As the settlers, Loyalists, and Native Americans descend on the mill, Ben Buck, his older sister, Annie, and Joe Mountain, the Bucks' young slave, hide in the cellar. After the fighting, they emerge to see a horrific scene:

> Father was still crouched by the hatchway as I popped up. "Don't come up here yet, Ben," he said. But it was too late. Isaac [Ben's brother-in-law] was lying by the mill door, on his face, and Mother was lying sort of on top of him, on her back, her eyes wide open and staring up at the roof. Both of them were scalped.[11]

Despite the massacre, Ben's father refuses to leave the Wyoming Valley. He even resists after American lawmakers decide in 1782 that the area belongs to Pennsylvania, giving the Pennsylvanians a legal basis to drive the Bucks off their land. Ben's father would rather fight them than return to Connecticut, where he would have no hope of owning his own land. He would have to work for wages on his brother's farm, which in his eyes would make him no better than a slave.

Much of the book's drama emerges from Ben's slow understanding of how his predicament mirrors Joe Mountain's. After the Wyoming Valley becomes part of Pennsylvania, Joe Mountain hears that he is free under Pennsylvania law. At first, Ben is discomforted by the idea that Joe is no longer a slave: "I didn't want Joe Mountain to be free. I wanted things to stay just the way they were. I knew it was a bad thing to want, but I couldn't help myself."[12] But over time, as he realizes returning to Connecticut would doom him to a life of servitude, Ben comes to understand and respect Joe's desire for freedom. Years later, the adult Ben concludes:

> The only lesson I found . . . is that it's hard as hell to spend your life never belonging to yourself. No one wants to be a slave, whether it's the

kind Joe Mountain was with a master who owned him, or the kind I almost got to be—having to work for somebody else with no chance of building something for myself.[13]

The Bloody Country was generally well received by critics. Many reviews applauded the rich relationship between Ben and Joe. *Booklist* held that "there's a noteworthy story thread that explores the relationship between Ben and their family slave Joe Mountain and functions to chart Ben's evolving belief that freedom belongs to all."[14] Its gritty depiction of pioneer life was also singled out for praise. For example, in *Washington Post Book World*, Olivia Coolidge wrote, "*The Bloody Country* is . . . dramatic, well-constructed . . . [and] gives a vivid picture of the hard work and persistence so often needed by the successful pioneer."[15]

In the book, the Colliers are also particularly successful at showing how careless use of natural resources could ultimately threaten settlers' lives and livelihoods. In *The Bloody Country*, Ben recalls that in Connecticut, settlers had cut down so many trees that there were few left. He admires the lushness of the Wyoming Valley but soon realizes that the pioneers are destroying its forests as well. The deforestation eventually leads to an ecological disaster—the great flood of 1787, which destroys the Bucks' mill and the homes of many of their neighbors. (Christopher Collier has sadly noted that people in the area learned little from this disaster. In 1975, a year before *The Bloody Country* was published, another flood caused in part by deforestation destroyed much of the region.)

Despite the critical success of *The Bloody Country*, James Lincoln Collier later had some reservations about the book. He felt that the action in *The Bloody Country* takes place over too long a period of time, making the story difficult to follow. "We struggled mightily to keep the story glued together,"[16] Collier conceded.

The Winter Hero

The Colliers' third collaboration, *The Winter Hero*, was published two years later. Narrated by twelve-year-old Justin Conkey, the novel has a much smaller scope, focusing on a conflict known as Shays's Rebellion (1786–1787).

Living with his sister, Molly, and his brother-in-law, Peter, Justin helps run a small farm in Massachusetts. However, their livelihood and that of their neighbors is placed in jeopardy by high taxes levied by the state's assembly. Like Peter, many of these farmers fought on the side of the patriots during the American Revolution. But the assembly members, mostly wealthy men, feel no obligation to help these veterans. And the farmers have no representatives in the assembly, since they did not raise the money needed to pay their salaries and expenses. Without political representation, Peter and other farmers conclude they can only combat the tax through rebellion.

From this conflict arises a central theme of *The Winter Hero*—what should citizens do when the government is not acting in their interest? Initially, Justin thinks of the rebellion in simple terms. He sees it largely as an opportunity to prove himself in battle: "The one thing I wanted, more than anything, was to do something glorious and brave so that Peter would admire me."[17]

Through the course of the book, Justin develops a more complex way of looking at the conflict. He begins questioning what responsibilities the government has toward its citizens. Molly suggests that he think of the government as the head of a household: "Peter gives you orders, but he's on your side, and trying to see that things go right for you . . . The one who's in charge ought to be looking out for everybody."[18] Later, his friend Levi offers a more bleak view. Levi is convinced a good government is impossible since anyone with power is likely to abuse it: "It's human nature for the rich to want to stay rich . . . and for the ones on the top to push on the ones below."[19]

But through his own experience, Justin begins to have even more profound doubts about the rebellion. The fiercest engagement is a disaster for the rebels. When they attack an arsenal, they are driven off by the better-armed Massachusetts army. Most of the rebels, including Justin, run away in terror. Justin is disappointed by his cowardice and at the same time loses faith in the rebellion. He also loses his enthusiasm for his old notions of heroism. Justin later saves Peter's life, and his fellow soldiers declare him a hero. But by the end of the book, he has come to see his action differently: "One thing I had learned was that there wasn't much point in going out to be a hero . . . You might as well go along and do your best, and not worry about who's the hero and who isn't."[20]

Unlike most of the Colliers' novels, *The Winter Hero* offers a fairly straightforward moral to the reader. In the end, the rebellion fails, but it does inspire the farmers to start sending their own representatives to the state assembly. As a result, they are able to change the tax laws, which allows them to keep their farms. According to Christopher Collier, the book's message is that "the price of liberty is more than eternal vigilance; keeping your rights requires some effort, too. Democracy does not work when the people do not play their part."[21] In simpler language, Justin himself spells out this point in the book's final chapter: "And one last thing that we learned out of it was that if you don't take the trouble to vote your own representatives to the government, the government is likely to do a lot of things you don't like."[22]

4 The Arabus Family Saga

The Colliers' third collaboration, *The Winter Hero*, was almost their last. It took many drafts to get it right. Christopher Collier became impatient with the amount of time the rewriting process took. He vowed he would never collaborate on another historical novel.

James Lincoln Collier, however, wanted to give it another try. He asked Christopher to reconsider, finally persuading his brother to spend just one day thinking about a subject he would like to explore. A few hours later, James got a call. Christopher had a new idea for a book. He suggested they again set the book in the Revolutionary War period. But this time, he wanted their narrator to be an African American teenager. Christopher Collier was excited by the chance to approach the slave experience from this perspective. There were many books for young adults about slaves in the South before the Civil War (1861–1865). But little was available about slaves in the North in the earliest days of the United States.

The Colliers began their work. Just a little more than a year later, they finished the manuscript for *Jump Ship to Freedom*. The book tells the story of Daniel Arabus, a slave from Connecticut who escapes to New York City aboard a merchant ship. The Colliers' editor liked the manuscript so much that she asked them to make it part of a trilogy. They agreed to write a prequel and a sequel. These would deal with the experiences of other members of the Arabus family before and after the events described in *Jump Ship*.

War Comes to Willy Freeman

Chronologically, the first of the three Arabus books is *War Comes to Willy Freeman* (1983). The "Willy" of the title is Wilhelmina Freeman. The story begins in Connecticut in 1781, when Willy's father, Jordan, is serving in the patriot army. Willy and her parents had once been slaves. But when Jordan Freeman enlisted, their master granted freedom not only to Freeman, but to his family as well.

Early in the novel, Willy's family is destroyed. She watches as her father is killed by British soldiers during the Battle of Groton. In the chaos after the battle, her mother disappears, presumably taken captive by the British. Alone, Willy heads off to New York City in search of her mother.

Willy Freeman is an adventure story about a courageous, clever heroine. But it is also an examination of how people's status in their society affects every aspect of their lives. Willy may be uneducated, but her narration reveals a sophisticated understanding of the world she lives in and her place in it.

Though no longer a slave, Willy knows she is not entirely free. In fact, her free status is constantly under threat. She has nothing to document her independence, forcing her to hide from Thomas Ivers, a ruthless sea captain who hopes to enslave her again if he can. Perhaps because her own liberty is constantly at risk, Willy values the principle of freedom all the more. As she puts it, "It was a funny thing to me how people wanted to be free. If you was scrubbing a floor for your own self in your own cabin, why, that was all right; it didn't hardly seem like work. But if you was scrubbing somebody else's floor, it was just awful."[1]

Slave or not, because Willy is African American, she has few rights in early America. But, as the Colliers make clear, her gender also places her at risk. The first of their novels narrated by a girl, *Willy Freeman* examines how, in Willy's day, being a female was not that different from being a slave. As Willy herself observes, "When you was a woman you was half a slave, anyway. You had to get married, otherwise you couldn't hardly support yourself, and after that your husband, he was the boss and you had to do what he said."[2] Willy also sadly acknowledges that the United States' new-found independence from England is unlikely to help her lot: "Slaves wasn't going to be no freer under the Americans than they was under the British, and women was still going to have to keep their place. I was black and I was a woman, and I knew there was limits."[3]

In many ways, *Willy Freeman* focuses on the heroine's powerlessness. Yet it also celebrates Willy as a girl with enormous daring and courage. Through grit and intelligence, she survives in New York while she searches for her mother. Upon learning that her dying mother is back in Connecticut, Willy risks her life and freedom to see her again. The novel ends on a note of optimism, as Willy comes to the aid of her uncle, Jack Arabus. Arabus was promised his freedom in exchange for serving in the American Revolution, but after the war, his master tried to keep him enslaved. In an episode based on an actual court case, Arabus sues his master and wins not only his own freedom but that of hundreds of other Connecticut slaves who fought in the Continental army.

Jump Ship to Freedom

The second book of the Arabus trilogy, *Jump Ship to Freedom*, begins in 1787, a few weeks after Jack Arabus's death. It focuses on his son, Daniel, who hopes to buy his and his mother's freedom. His father left them notes worth $600—the payment for his military service. At the time, though, the United States, after giving up on the Articles of Confederation, is in the process of forming a new government under the Constitution. This new government will decide whether it would honor the notes. If it does not, the notes will be worthless, and Daniel's dreams of buying his way out of slavery will be destroyed. In this way, the Colliers tie Daniel's fate to the fate of the United States.

For the authors, placing the drafting of the Constitution at the center of a novel seemed natural. Christopher Collier has spent much of his career as a historian studying the event. Both Colliers later collaborated on a nonfiction book for adults— *Decision in Philadelphia: The Constitutional Convention of 1787* (1986)—detailing how the Constitution was written.

During the novel, Daniel escapes from his master and hides in New York, then the capital of the United States. Still on the run, he flees the city with Peter Fatherscreft, a delegate traveling to the Constitutional Convention in Philadelphia. When Fatherscreft dies, Daniel must make a decision about whether to fulfill a deathbed promise he made. Fatherscreft asked Daniel to relay a message to the convention members, suggesting a compromise on the issue of slavery.

The drafters of the Constitution were not considering abolishing slavery. They were, however, divided about how to deal with fugitive slaves and the foreign slave trade. One central disagreement was whether the new United States should allow the continued importation of slaves. Fatherscreft's compromise was aimed at calming certain Southern states, whose representatives were balking at any talk of restricting slavery. Fatherscreft proposed, for example, a provision that allowed for the slave trade to continue at least for the next twenty years. He hoped the Southern states would accept his compromises and therefore agree to ratify the Constitution. The situation sets up the book's central irony. If Daniel delivers the message, he is helping further the cause of slavery. If he does not, the Constitutional Convention might fail, and the United States might fall apart.

Another source of drama in *Jump Ship* occurs in Daniel's mind. At first, Daniel worries he is not smart enough to win his freedom. Raised in a racist world, he accepts the idea that, as an African American, he is not as intelligent, brave, or honest as white people. Throughout his adventures, however, Daniel displays all these qualities. Through his admirable behavior, the Colliers show readers that, despite living in a society that undervalues him, Daniel grows up to become a good and decent man. Slowly, even Daniel comes to question what his society has taught him. Through his own experiences, he discovers that race has nothing to do with a person's worth. As he tells Fatherscreft: "I've been looking at the whole thing pretty hard the past little while, and it seems to me that there ain't much difference one way or another . . . Take the skin off of us, and it would be pretty hard to tell which was the white ones and which ones wasn't."[4] He also dismisses the notion behind slavery—that human beings can be bought and sold. At one point, Daniel says: "Well, I guess a man's life don't exactly measure out in money. I mean, what's the use of having the money, if you don't have your life?"[5]

Who Is Carrie?

While in New York, Daniel befriends a little girl he nicknames Nosey. She reappears as the narrator of *Who Is Carrie?* (1984). This final book in the Arabus trilogy takes place in 1789 in New York, where the U.S. Constitution was adopted as the law of the land.

Carrie is one of the Colliers' liveliest narrators. As a reviewer wrote in *Publishers Weekly*, "Carrie . . . tells her story in a comic, moving fashion that creates empathy in the reader."[6] Laboring as a slave in New York's famous Fraunces Tavern, Carrie has a wit and curiosity that enlivens a story that otherwise might be a grim read.

In many ways, Carrie has a clearer understanding of her self-worth from the beginning than either

Willy or Daniel. Despite her lowly status, she respects herself. She is confident enough to joke about the injustice of her world.

But underlying her good humor is a deep sorrow. Carrie does not know where she came from or who her parents are. Her unknown history makes her feel incomplete. As she explains: "Oh, it was hard not knowing where I came from. I didn't even have no last name. I was a mystery to myself . . . If you didn't know who you was, you wasn't nobody. There ain't nothing much worse than being nobody."[7] Carrie's vivid imagination, however, does at least provide her with some relief. In one particularly poignant instance, she explains that by imagining she is a bird, she often escapes her troubles for a moment, at least in her mind: "I'd wonder what it would be like to be able to fly away to wherever you wanted—up on top of a roof or into a church steeple, or just go away, way up and look down . . . I'd give anything to have wings. I'd fly away and never be a slave no more."[8] Christopher Collier has pointed out that Carrie's ignorance of her personal history makes her a metaphor for all African American slaves. Forcibly taken from their African homelands, they, like Carrie, lost a sense of the connection between their past and their present.

James Lincoln Collier feels that, through *Carrie*, he was able to correct a flaw in the other two Arabus books. In writing the trilogy, the Colliers set out to create a historically accurate picture of African American life in the late eighteenth century. But, as James found, writing about slaves poses a problem. Since slaves had little power over their lives, it is difficult to write action-filled stories about them. In *Willy Freeman* and *Jump Ship*, James solved this problem by making both of the protagonists runaways. But, in fact, very few slaves actually ran away, so their stories are hardly representative of the experiences of most African Americans at the time. In *Carrie*, James decided that Carrie should remain enslaved throughout the book. (Even so, as Christopher has noted, she is treated much better at the tavern where she works than most slaves of the day would be.)

In several drafts, James Lincoln Collier gave *Carrie* a happy ending, in which she discovered papers proving who her parents were. But neither James nor Christopher felt this ending worked. It seemed too upbeat and too tidy a conclusion to Carrie's story. In the end, James reworked the last pages of the book to make Carrie's situation less certain. She comes to suspect she is Daniel Arabus's cousin and as such is legally free. But without documentation, she will never know for sure. The situation tries even Carrie's good humor. The story's final lines express her frustration: "It isn't fair, Dan. It isn't fair."[9] In a few simple words, Carrie boils down the pain of the African American experience explored throughout the Colliers' trilogy.

5 Censoring History

T he Collier brothers have won many awards for their work. But there is one book list they would prefer not to be on. The American Library Association (ALA) compiled a list of the 100 "most frequently challenged books" from 1990 to 2000. The Colliers made the list twice. *Jump Ship to Freedom* was number 100, while *My Brother Sam Is Dead* made it all the way to number 12. The ALA defines a challenge as "an attempt to remove or restrict materials, based upon the objections of a person or group."[1]

Language and Violence

Most often, the people trying to pull the Colliers' books from library shelves have been parents. One of their most common complaints is that some of the Colliers' characters, even children, drink alcohol. But the Colliers point out that drinking was an accepted part of life in eighteenth-century America. To leave alcohol out of the books entirely would misrepresent the era. Similarly, some people have complained that the Colliers' female characters are not assertive enough. Again, the authors argue that, in the past, American women enjoyed far less freedom than they do today. They were expected to submit to the will of their fathers and their husbands.

However, the most frequent objection to the Colliers' work is that it includes profane language. In Colorado in 1996, for instance, one grandmother challenged *My Brother Sam* after visiting her granddaughter's fifth-grade classroom. As the students were taking turns reading the book, the grandmother was offended by the curse words spoken by some of the characters. She lodged a complaint, demanding that the book be removed from the school library. She told a reporter, "Students don't have to read stuff like that. Don't tell me I'm doing censorship. I'm just asking that what they're doing in the public realm to be acceptable to everyone."[2] In another challenge to *My Brother Sam*, a Pennsylvania school board responded by blacking out the offending words and phrases in students' copies. One official defended the decision, explaining, "We decided that the swear words really added nothing to the book."[3]

The Colliers disagree. They maintain that profanity in their books serves a dual purpose. It helps make the books historically accurate, since profane words would have been part of their characters' vocabulary. And it also aids them in storytelling. As Christopher Collier explains:

> Students will learn nothing from [our books] unless they read them. They won't read them . . . unless the story engages, interests and excites them . . . Strongly connotative, colorful, and striking words are a major literary tool to create character, context, and their inter-relationships, all to bring about real historical understanding.[4]

The violence in *My Brother Sam* has also been a source of controversy. Particularly disturbing to some parents is the description of Sam's execution:

> He hit the ground on his belly and flopped over on his back. He wasn't dead yet. He lay there shaking and thrashing about, his knees jerking up and down. They had shot him from so close that his clothes were on fire. He went

on jerking with flames on his chest until another soldier shot him again. Then he stopped jerking.[5]

In a 1999 challenge of the book, one mother in Oak Brook, Illinois, said her sixth-grade son was upset by the death scene. "I don't think it's necessary or appropriate for that grade level,"[6] she insisted.

Views of the Revolution

A few attacks on *My Brother Sam* have concentrated on its view of the Revolutionary War era. In Cheshire, Connecticut, in 1991, parents complained about the book because of its "graphic violence" and "inaccurate depiction of the Revolutionary War."[7] They made their objections only a few months after Christopher Collier, then the official state historian of Connecticut, came to the defense of two other books the town's parents had tried to ban.

Claims that *My Brother Sam* is inaccurate draw largely from the fact that the narrative does not conform to popular ideas about the Revolution and why it was fought. Soon after *My Brother Sam*'s publication, Christopher Collier anticipated this type of complaint in an essay published in the *Horn Book Magazine* titled "Johnny and Sam: Old and

New Approaches to the American Revolution." Intended for teachers, the essay describes how theories about the Revolution have changed over time. Initially, historians of the era maintained that the colonists fought largely on principle. In order to live as free men, they were willing to fight and die. All too often, this view of the war is still taught in schools. It is also promoted in Esther Forbes's *Johnny Tremain* (1943). Until *My Brother Sam*, this book was the best-known young adult novel about the Revolution.

By the early twentieth century, Collier notes in his essay, serious historians had come to view the war differently. They saw it as a conflict initiated by colonial leaders for their economic and political gain. He writes, "The American War for Independence was only part of a civil war that pitted brother against brother as aristocratic and popular interests struggled to control the policy-making machinery of their respective colonies."[8] In *My Brother Sam*, the Colliers wanted to present this more complex view of the war. They especially wanted to dramatize how everyday people were swept up into this struggle, often against their will.

African American Issues

Some of the most fevered challenges of the Colliers' novels have focused on the Arabus trilogy.

The use of the word "nigger" is a common complaint. While acknowledging this word is offensive to today's readers, the Colliers maintain the word is necessary for the sake of historical accuracy. During the late eighteenth century, African American slaves were routinely referred to as "niggers" by others and by themselves. In addition, as Christopher Collier has noted, their "use of the N word is intended to deepen the depiction of the misery of slavery and of the degraded status of free blacks as well."[9]

Ironically, the Colliers' desire to present an honest depiction of racism in America has angered some African Americans. In one case, *Jump Ship to Freedom* was challenged when a sixth-grader told his teacher he was offended by the novel after reading just the first chapter. The student was disturbed by Daniel Arabus's sense of racial inferiority, revealed in passages such as: "I knew that black folks were supposed to be more stupid than white folks; that was God's way, the minister said. Black folks were meant to do the work, and white folks the thinking. If God had made black folks smart, they'd have got restless about doing the hard work."[10] Several parents wanted the book removed from all the libraries in the county's grade schools. The school superintendent, though, refused. As the assistant superintendent explained, "The irony is, if you read the whole book the boy concludes that he is as smart as whites. He prevails against all odds and he gets his money back. The book in its totality is very affirming of blacks."[11]

In another case, *War Comes to Willy Freeman* was challenged in a school outside of Chicago, Illinois. A parent complained that the book promoted a negative view of African Americans and was therefore inappropriate for children. She cited several passages, in which Willy acknowledges the inferior status she suffers as a female African American slave. For example, one passage deemed offensive was from a scene in which Willy is walking through New York City at night in the disguise of a boy: "Some people looked at us, but they didn't pay us no mind. We were just a couple of black boys, and wasn't worth more than a glance."[12]

James Lincoln Collier made a case for the book in a letter to the editor of the *Chicago Star*. He wrote, "By far the majority of black parents and educators believe that their students ought to be given a realistic view of the horrors of slavery. We will do nothing to ameliorate [better] conditions for blacks if we pretend that those conditions do not exist."[13] But, despite its eloquence, his argument fell on deaf ears. As often happens when one of the Colliers' books is challenged, the school district decided to remove *Willy Freeman* from the shelves of its libraries.

6 A Prolific Author

As a children's author, James Lincoln Collier remains best known for the novels of the Revolutionary War that he wrote with his brother. But Collier has written many more books for young people. Some are historical novels like *My Brother Sam*. Others are novels with young heroes in contemporary settings. And others are nonfiction works, meant to teach and inform readers about a subject.

James Lincoln Collier is proud of his ability to write in so many different styles and on so many different subjects. To him, such versatility is a sign of his professionalism. It certainly has helped to make him one of the most prolific authors for young readers. Including the works he has coauthored, Collier has written more than 100 books.

The Collaboration Continues

After the Arabus family saga, the Collier brothers collaborated on two more novels. *The Clock* (1991) tells the story of Annie Steele, whose dreams of becoming a teacher are dashed when her father sends her to work in a factory. The book takes place in 1810, just as factories were becoming a part of American life.

Annie faces enormous struggles both at work and at home. In the factory, she has to fight off the advances of her boss, Mr. Hoggart. In her family, she has to fight for any say over her life, during a time when children, especially girls, were expected to obey their fathers no matter what. The clock in the title is an expensive gadget Annie's father brings home as the book begins. Already deep in debt, he gleefully shows off his new acquisition. But as Annie quickly learns, she is the one who will have to pay for it by working at a difficult and dangerous job. Annie clearly spells out the powerlessness she feels in her society: "I'd come to be everybody's toy, for them to play with as they liked."[1]

The Colliers next wrote *With Every Drop of Blood* (1994), set during the American Civil War.

(The title was adapted from a line in President Abraham Lincoln's second inaugural address.) Like the Arabus family saga, the story deals with racism in American society. But this novel is narrated by a white Southern boy named Johnny, who has been told all his life that whites are superior to blacks. After his father dies fighting for the Confederacy, Johnny sets out on an adventure. He joins a caravan carrying supplies to Confederate troops. On the way, the caravan is attacked by Union soldiers. Much to his shock, Johnny is taken prisoner by Cush, an African American boy about his age.

Like Daniel in *Jump Ship to Freedom*, Johnny comes to reexamine his ideas about race through the course of the novel. At first, he is humiliated that Cush has power over him. But over time, the two boys become friends as they travel together and are forced to rely on one another in order to survive the final days of the war. Johnny not only comes to respect Cush's humanity, but, just as Daniel does, Johnny also eventually accepts a more universal truth—a person is truly defined by his character, not by his race.

More recently, the Colliers collaborated on an ambitious nonfiction work—the Drama of American History series. Composed of twenty-three volumes, this series is a complete history of the United States for young readers. Reviewers have praised the Colliers' skill at explaining complicated ideas in clear and entertaining language. As Carolyn Phelan wrote in *Booklist*, "Few nonfiction series books for young people could be read one after the other with more enjoyment and enlightenment than these."[2]

Hard Times

Working without Christopher, James Lincoln Collier has recently written a series of biographies for children. Called the You Never Knew series, these books get behind the myths about the lives of famous people, exploring both their strengths and their shortcomings. The subjects include men and women from throughout the history of the United States—from Benjamin Franklin to Sitting Bull to Eleanor Roosevelt. Further showing his diverse interests, Collier has written several other nonfiction books on a variety of topics, including vaccines and the history of clocks.

Since he began his career, Collier has also written on his own more than a dozen novels for young readers. Among them are several works of historical fiction. The first was *My Crooked Family* (1991), which explores the bleak side of city life in the early twentieth century. In the opening scene, the narrator, Roger, is nearly arrested for stealing dinner for himself and his little sister, and his father, a petty criminal, ends up in the hospital after being shot. During his father's recovery, Roger struggles to care for his family. Collier shows the desperation of the urban poor as Roger finds himself, like his father, drawn into a life of crime.

Collier returned to this setting in *Chipper* (2001), which was named a Notable Social Studies Trade Book for Young People in 2002. Set in 1895 in New York City, the book focuses on thirteen-year-old Chipper, a member of a gang of poor children living on the streets. The novel ultimately turns into a mystery tale. When a wealthy woman begins oddly taking an interest in Chipper, he starts to suspect there are secrets he does not know about his family and where he came from.

The struggles of the poor are also a theme of *The Worst of Times: A Story of the Great Depression* (2000). The novel is set during the Great Depression of the 1930s—a time when high unemployment plunged many American families into poverty. The novel's hero, Petey Williamson, watches his family suffer greatly before becoming involved in a labor union demanding more protections for workers.

Collier often takes the side of the downtrodden in his fiction. But *The Worst of Times* paints a particularly brutal picture of how the have-nots suffer in a world where the haves enjoy most of the power.

After writing many novels about the American Revolution, Collier for the first time explored the very beginnings of America in *The Corn Raid: A Story of Jamestown* (2000). Its protagonist, Richard Ayre, is an English orphan. In the early seventeenth century, he is sent to live in the Jamestown settlement in the colony of Virginia. Like the Arabus trilogy, *The Corn Raid* deals with racism, though, in this novel, its victims are the Native Americans that white colonists encountered in North America.

Family Matters

One of Collier's best recent novels is *Wild Boy* (2002). A historical novel set in the early nineteenth century, it is narrated by twelve-year-old Jesse, who lives alone in the wilderness. Jesse wants to become a mountain man—one of a rough breed of men who made their living by trapping animals and trading their furs. The novel illustrates just how hard it was to live on the American frontier. Even with the help of a friendly trapper, Jesse struggles to keep from going hungry and to build a house warm enough to survive the winter.

Wild Boy also highlights one of Collier's favorite themes—the conflicts adolescents have with their parents as they become more independent and develop a sense of their own identity. Jesse comes to live in the woods after a terrible fight he has with his father. After hitting Pa in a fit of rage, Jesse believes he will never be able to go home again. But his troubles force him to grow up fast, and soon Jesse sees Pa's love for him is not so easily destroyed. He also discovers that making his own way in the world, without the love of family, is not as easy as he thought it would be.

Collier has also written several novels about contemporary families. Like Jesse, the narrator of *Outside Looking In* (1987) decides the only way to deal with his difficult father is to run away. Fergy at fourteen grows tired of his family's way of life. Living out of a van, his parents refuse to work, and his father has no trouble stealing when times are tough. Fergy rebels by taking off for his grandparents' house. During the adventure, he is finally able to come to terms with his parents' unconventional lives.

Collier's protagonists often struggle to cope with their family's lack of wealth. Chris in *The Winchesters* (1988), as a less well-off member of the wealthy Winchester clan, finds himself feeling like an outsider in his own family. Harry in *When the Stars Begin to Fall* (1986) is desperate to make a name for himself, since his town has branded his poor family as "trash." In these books, Collier tries to help young readers sort through their own difficult relationships with others by reading about the protagonists' struggles to solve similar problems. What a reviewer for *Booklist* wrote about *When the Stars Begin to Fall* could be said of many of Collier's novels: "Collier's story is designed to make readers think about the complexity of some moral issues and about matters of honor and truth."[3]

7 Making Music

James Lincoln Collier is not just a writer. He is also a musician. For about fifty years, he has worked part-time, playing trombone in jazz bands in New York City. For Collier, music and writing have much in common. His two passions tap similar creative instincts within him. As he says, "Both require me to perform, using my imagination, my feelings, and a sound grasp of the techniques of the craft."[1]

Advice for Young Musicians

From the start of his book-writing career, Collier encouraged young readers to learn more about music. He wrote one book about choosing an instrument (*Which Musical Instrument Shall I Play?*; 1969) and another about understanding musical theory (*Practical Music Theory: How Music Is Put Together from Bach to Rock*; 1970). For teenagers interested in making a living as a musician, Collier offered *Making Music for Money* (1976), a comprehensive guide on how to form a band. Although it was published about thirty years ago, it is full of practical advice, much of which is still useful today. It explains how to recruit band members, how to develop a distinctive sound, and how to get and publicize paying gigs.

In the book, Collier draws on his own experiences as an aspiring trombone player. To emphasize how important formal training is, he describes the pitfalls he fell into without it: "When I was a teenager I took up the trombone in order to improvise jazz. I never bothered to take any lessons. I just taught myself, partly out of a book, and partly just by hook and by crook. Eventually I was good enough to play in some small jazz bands, but the truth is that I wasn't really very good." Taking "serious lessons from a first-rate teacher" allowed him to become "a much better jazz trombonist" as well as a more "well-rounded musician."[2]

A Jazz Historian

A few of Collier's early books for young readers reflect his love of jazz. *Inside Jazz* (1973) is an introduction to this style of music. In the *New York Times Book Review*, Loraine Alterman raved, "[Collier] provides as good a verbal explanation as I've seen about jazz."[3] *The Great Jazz Artists* (1977) features biographies of jazz masters, including Jelly Roll Morton, Louis Armstrong, Billie Holiday, and Charlie Parker.

Perhaps Collier's best writing for adults has been on jazz history. In the jazz world, the publication of *The Making of Jazz: A Comprehensive History* (1978) was an important event. The music critic John McDonough wrote in *Down Beat* magazine that Collier's book was the best history of jazz to appear in print for twenty years. McDonough went on to praise the book for making jazz accessible to newcomers to the music, while noting that it also had plenty of information of interest to jazz experts as well.

In the 1980s, Collier also made a splash with adult biographies of three leading figures in jazz— Louis Armstrong, Benny Goodman, and Duke Ellington. All prompted a debate among serious jazz fans, but his biography of Ellington was especially controversial. Some criticized Collier for discussing some of the less admirable aspects of Ellington's personality and for dismissing his longer compositions. Nevertheless, his scholarly books about these musical giants have stood the test of time. They remain classics of American music writing.

Drawing on the years of research needed to produce these lengthy adult books, Collier has more recently written shorter versions for his younger fans. The young adult biographies *Louis Armstrong: An American Success Story* (1985) and *Duke Ellington* (1991) discuss the music of these two jazz greats and explain the difficulties they faced as African Americans in a music business largely run by whites. Even more ambitious was *Jazz: An American Saga* (1997)—a complete history of jazz in only 112 pages. Throughout the book, Collier challenges the jazz fan's tendency to celebrate only one style, denouncing all others as not really jazz. Collier instead invites listeners new to jazz to learn to appreciate the music's many genres—from Dixieland to bop to fusion.

Music and Fiction

Music plays an important part not only in Collier's nonfiction but also in many of his novels for young readers. In these books, he explores both the joys of playing music and the struggles many musicians face when trying to make a living from their art.

Collier takes a comic look at the problems of an aspiring musician in his first novel, *The Teddy Bear Habit*. The book's hero, George Stable, is one of Collier's funniest narrators. He aspires to be a rock star, even though his father hates rock and insists George instead study singing with a serious voice teacher. Behind his father's back, George takes guitar lessons and lands a spot playing on a television special.

The Teddy Bear Habit was successful enough to inspire a sequel, *Rich and Famous: The Further Adventures of George Stable* (1975). In this novel, Collier again pokes fun of the music industry, particularly its preference for image over talent. A record company decides to make a star out of George. They invent a new country-boy image for him—"George Stable, the Boy Next Door"—even though he has lived all his life in Manhattan. Collier also looked at the seamier side of the popular music industry in *Rock Star* (1970). The novel's protagonist, Tim, is so devoted to playing music that he runs away to New York City, but he finds that pursuing his dream is far more difficult than he had hoped. The book was named one of the best books of the year by the Child Study Children's Book Committee.

In two music-themed novels, Collier explored his love of jazz. In *Give Dad My Best* (1976), set in the Great Depression, it is not his young protagonist Jack who is the musician. It is instead Jack's father that has the all-absorbing love of music. A trombonist like Collier himself, Jack's father is so consumed by his music that he ignores the needs of his family, laying that uncomfortable burden on Jack. In the *New York Times*, reviewer Joyce Bermel pointed out, "What gives the novel its distinctive texture is not the son's imaginings but the father's love affair with music. The care he denies his children, he lavishes on his trombone. Money earmarked for food, he squanders on records."[4]

The hero of *The Jazz Kid* (1994) is similarly obsessed with jazz. Although the novel is set in Chicago during the 1920s, Collier probably modeled the protagonist Paulie at least partly after himself. Like Collier in his youth, Paulie at first is determined to teach himself to play jazz on his own. But he only becomes a skillful musician after he gets instruction from a seasoned band teacher and a professional musician who takes Paulie under his wing. Collier, too, must have been remembering his own early experiences when Paulie describes his first encounter with the music he comes to love:

> It didn't really matter what the tune was. What counted was the way that music felt to me, the sparkle that was in it, the funny way it scurried along, going here and there, disappearing behind something and then popping out again. I couldn't believe music could make you feel that way.[5]

In Paulie's words, Collier expresses his own passion for jazz. But, unlike his character, playing music is only one of many hobbies. As he explains: "I have many interests. I play jazz regularly, like sports, read a great deal, cook, travel a lot, and enjoy working around my country house."[6]

Writing, however, is different for Collier. It is not just something he enjoys—it is something he is driven to do. In fact, he considers it the most important thing in his life. "Writing is always first," he once wrote. "It is the thing on which everything else depends. It is at the center of my life, and I cannot imagine not doing it."[7]

Interview with James Lincoln Collier

LIZ SONNEBORN: You've spoken of your self-discipline as a writer. Can you discuss some of your working habits? Do you write every day for certain hours? Do you write so many words a day?

JAMES LINCOLN COLLIER: I write five and sometimes six days a week, starting at 7 AM, for five or six hours.

LIZ SONNEBORN: What incidents from your adolescence have most deeply affected your life? Have these incidents shaped your fiction for young adults in any way?

JAMES LINCOLN COLLIER: I came from a family that had been bookish for many generations, and at various times had been connected to illustrious American literary figures. My life was conditioned by this fact. I have always been deeply concerned about books and writing.

LIZ SONNEBORN: How has your writing been influenced by your interest in music? To you, how does the act of writing compare to the act of playing the trombone?

JAMES LINCOLN COLLIER: My interest in music led me to writing many books and articles about jazz, among them some scholarly works on jazz rhythm.

LIZ SONNEBORN: After years of collaborating with your brother, Christopher, you've recently written a number of historical novels on your own. How do you get the ideas for your own historical novels? How do you go about researching these books?

JAMES LINCOLN COLLIER: For my historical novels, I choose a subject that will interest me and will be of use to teachers. My research is the usual stuff—I read scholarly books and papers on the subject and visit appropriate places as much as possible.

LIZ SONNEBORN: How do you feel about efforts to ban your books, particularly *My Brother Sam Is Dead*?

JAMES LINCOLN COLLIER: I am not as touchy about banning attempts as some authors. Mostly they have had little effect. I believe that if the parents of a town don't want their kids reading my books, they have a right to keep them out of the schools. However, it must be a majority, not a noisy minority.

LIZ SONNEBORN: Many of your novels deal with relationships between fathers and sons. How have your own experiences as a son and as a father influenced your portrayal of the father-son relationship?

JAMES LINCOLN COLLIER: I did not get along with my father very well and it shows in some of my books, but certainly not in all of them.

LIZ SONNEBORN: Your Drama of American History series covers the entire history of the United States. What do you see as the most important lesson (or lessons) young people can take from the study of American history?

JAMES LINCOLN COLLIER: The Drama of American History series, if it comes to one point, is that the price of liberty is eternal vigilance.

LIZ SONNEBORN: Which of your books was the most difficult to write, and why?

JAMES LINCOLN COLLIER: All are difficult.

LIZ SONNEBORN: What projects are you working on now? Are there any books you've been burning to write or new subjects you're interested in writing about for the first time?

JAMES LINCOLN COLLIER: I'm working on a historical novel for kids about the Russian Revolution. I'm also involved with a history of jazz in Europe.

LIZ SONNEBORN: What advice would you give to young aspiring writers?

JAMES LINCOLN COLLIER: If writing isn't as serious as religion to you, forget about it.

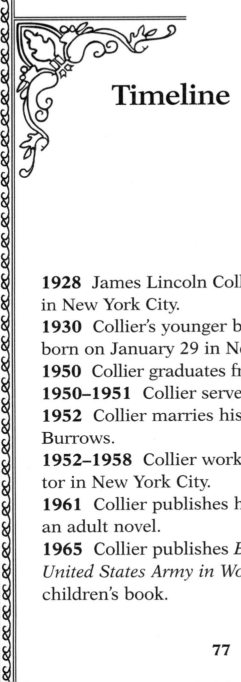

Timeline

1928 James Lincoln Collier is born on June 27 in New York City.

1930 Collier's younger brother, Christopher, is born on January 29 in New York City.

1950 Collier graduates from Hamilton College.

1950–1951 Collier serves in the U.S. Army.

1952 Collier marries his first wife, Carol Burrows.

1952–1958 Collier works as a magazine editor in New York City.

1961 Collier publishes his first book, *Cheers*, an adult novel.

1965 Collier publishes *Battleground: The United States Army in World War II*, his first children's book.

1967 Collier publishes his first novel for children, *The Teddy Bear Habit*.

1974 James Lincoln Collier and Christopher Collier publish their first collaboration, *My Brother Sam Is Dead*.

1975 *My Brother Sam Is Dead* is named a Newbery Honor Book.

1976 The Collier brothers publish *The Bloody Country*.

1978 The Colliers publish *The Winter Hero*. James Lincoln Collier publishes *The Making of Jazz: A Comprehensive History*. This controversial history of jazz in America is a finalist for the American Book Award.

1981 The Collier brothers publish *Jump Ship to Freedom*, the first book completed in the Arabus family trilogy.

1983 Collier marries his second wife, Ida Karen Potash. Collier receives critical acclaim for his adult biography *Louis Armstrong: An American Genius*. The Collier brothers publish *War Comes to Willy Freeman*.

1984 The Colliers complete the Arabus trilogy with *Who Is Carrie?*

1986 The Colliers collaborate on *Decision in Philadelphia: The Constitutional Convention of 1787*, a work of history for adults.

1994 Collier publishes *The Jazz Kid*. The Colliers win a Phoenix Award for *My Brother Sam Is Dead*. The award honors a children's book that has stood the test of time.

1998–2002 Benchmark Books publishes the Colliers' twenty-three-volume Drama of American History series.

2000 Collier publishes *The Corn Raid: A Story of Jamestown* and *The Worst of Times: A Story of the Great Depression*.

2004 Collier begins publishing the You Never Knew series of biographies for children.

Selected
Reviews from
School Library
Journal

The Bloody Country
May 1976

Gr 7 Up—Like the authors' Newbery Honor Book, *My Brother Sam Is Dead* (Four Winds: Scholastic, 1975), this is a compelling historical novel set during the Revolutionary War Period. The young narrator is caught in the midst of an agonizing struggle between Connecticut farmers who have settled along the fertile banks of the Susquehanna River and the native Pennsylvanians who are fiercely determined to drive them out. For the boy's father, his right to remain on his own land is sacred, and he stubbornly refuses to return to Connecticut and go to work for someone else.

After his mother and brother are brutally murdered, their legal right to the land denied in court, and their possessions destroyed by flood, the boy painfully questions his father's resolve to sacrifice everything for the sake of retaining his property. In ironic contrast, the boy's best friend, a half-Black and half-Indian boy who has been raised as the family's slave, leaves their home in Pennsylvania to secure his own freedom. The parallel between what freedom means for his friend and what the land symbolizes for his father is powerfully drawn in this intense and absorbing story.

The Clock
February 1992

Gr 6–8—Once again the Colliers have teamed up to write solid, well-researched, exciting historical fiction. Annie Steel, 15, lives in Connecticut in 1810, where the new textile mill heralds the beginning of a new age. Her spendthrift father, unable to resist such purchases as the newly invented clock, gets deeply in debt, and Annie must go to work in the mill. There she fends off the sexual advances of the cruel overseer who physically abuses the workers, even causing the death of Annie's disabled friend. When she discovers that the man is a thief, she bravely exposes him. In an addendum, the Colliers pose the question of whether or not progress—in this case the switch from "sun time to clock time"—is always for the better. Annie is a memorable character whose presence serves to point out the limited options available to women at that time. Fact and fiction are skillfully blended in this fast-paced, thought-provoking look at early 19th-century New England.

The Jazz Kid
June 1994

Gr 6–9—It is 1923 and Paulie Horvath, 13, wants to play the cornet more than anything. When he hears a jazz group practice, he's hooked. The music sweetly draws him in and won't let go. His school-work is ignored, and every spare minute is spent in secret practice sessions with a professional musician who befriends him. When the boy fails every subject, his disapproving father takes the precious horn away. Paulie runs away and becomes involved in Chicago's world of jazz clubs, low life, and gangsters. Eventually his obsession involves the family and his father must come to the rescue when some gang-sters make trouble. Paulie gratefully returns home, wiser and ready to take up his horn again more responsibly. Told in the first person, this is historical fiction that may need a little booktalking, but is well worth the push. The world of 1920's Chicago jazz comes alive through Paulie's eyes and ears. Famous musicians like the Rhythm Kings, King Oliver, Bix Beiderbecke, and others were part of a new and exciting era of sound. The "nigger music," as many whites called it, was greeted with mixed reactions; this becomes a perfect background for Paulie's dilemma. Collier writes with accurate detail and creates believable, realistic characters. Paulie's infatuation with the jazz sound is so clearly written, one can almost hear the horn singing. The multiple themes of music, family, and responsibility harmonize to make one fine story. An author's note gives listening suggestions and background information.

Jump Ship to Freedom
October 1981

Gr 4–7—Because Jack Arabus, a slave, had served in the American Revolution he had achieved freedom. He intended to buy the freedom of wife and son Daniel with his army pay, given in Continental notes. Before Jack could complete his plans, he was drowned at sea. His unscrupulous former master, Captain Ivers, had stolen the vital notes, and it was up to young Daniel to retrieve them. When the boy did so, he found himself aboard a ship bound for the West Indies, friendless and in trouble. Daniel's independence and self-esteem grow along with the boy's ability to maneuver out of dangerous situations. Not a polemic against slavery, nor the faithful recreation of a troubled period in American history, this is, first and foremost, an adventure. The period seems well researched, and the speech has an authentic ring without trying to imitate a dialect. (The use of the modern-sounding phrase "a piece of cake" is the one minor, but grating, anachronism in evidence).

War Comes to Willy Freeman
April 1983

Gr 6 Up—Once again the Colliers deal with the impact of war on humanity. The protagonist is feisty Willy Freeman, strong-minded and independent at a time when to be both a female and black meant double bondage. After seeing her father killed, Willy travels to New York in search of her mother, captured by the British. The nature of the book, a fast-paced adventure, precludes extensive character development. Willy is an endearing creature, though, and her exploits and daring ensure exciting reading. The Colliers certainly have a gift for using dialect realistically without it becoming obtrusive, although the sometimes use of the word "nigger" by both blacks and whites (explained in a helpful postscript) may offend modern sensibilities. More disturbing to some readers may be the fact that although Willy bemoans woman's lot as unequal and unfair—the authors acknowledge she may sound too modern— she twice uses the fact of her gender to save her life. A companion volume, this precedes *Jump Ship to Freedom* (Delacorte, 1981).

Who Is Carrie?
May 1984

Gr 5–8—A companion volume to *Jump Ship to Freedom* (Delacorte, 1981) and *War Comes to Willy Freeman* (Delacorte, 1983), *Who Is Carrie?* is another adventure-filled journey into the black experience of late 18th-Century America. Via a sensitive and insightful treatment, readers can vicariously experience the life and plight of blacks at this time. A young kitchen maid at Fraunces' tavern in New York City, Carrie becomes involved not only in a search for her own identity and status but in Dan Arabus's quest for freedom. At the conclusion, Carrie's future remains for all purposes uncertain and her situation unresolved, much the same as the status of slavery as a whole. Noteworthy historic figures such as George Washington and a backdrop of the new government, including the birth pains of the new nation and concerns of its leadership are skillfully inter-woven into the story of Carrie's search, yet her plight remains foremost in intensity. This is historical fiction at its best. The Colliers' familiar "How Much of This Book Is True" addendum fills readers in on the essentials concerning fictional and factual elements of the plot, as well as the research involved in its composition. Useful application in a middle grades black history curriculum or simply for enjoyable reading that provides a look at the life and times in late 18th-Century America.

The Winchesters
January 1989

Gr 6–9—Chris Winchester, a poor relation of a powerful family that controls their company town, lives with his widowed mother and younger siblings in the gatehouse to the Winchester estate, and finds that he has divided loyalties between the family and the town. Now, with wages being cut and the union threatening to strike, emotions are running high. Chris is implicated in an "us versus them" incident, and he finds himself alienated from his best friend and his girlfriend. Retribution escalates until Chris confronts his grandfather and uncle and successfully negotiates his own terms of justice. Collier depicts Chris Winchester as a boy in a modern setting whose life is very much influenced by history, in this case the Depression. He successfully describes the discomfort of a boy caught in the middle of a social dilemma. Chris is not unlike two recent Collier protagonists, Fergie from *Outside Looking In* (Macmillan, 1987) and Harry White of *When the Stars Begin to Fall* (Delacorte, 1986), who also battle moral issues involving wealth and social conscience. Readers will identify with his desire to give up his doubts about his family and to enjoy the spoils of their wealth, but they will also applaud him in his final confrontations with them. A solid Collier offering.

List of Selected Works

Battleground: The United States Army in World War II. New York, NY: W. W. Norton, 1965.

The Bloody Country (coauthored with Christopher Collier). Bristol, FL: Four Winds, 1976.

Chipper. New York, NY: Marshall Cavendish, 2001.

The Clock (coauthored with Christopher Collier). New York, NY: Delacorte, 1991.

The Corn Raid: A Story of the Jamestown Settlement. Lincolnwood, IL: Jamestown Publishers, 2000.

Danny Goes to the Hospital. New York, NY: W. W. Norton, 1970.

Decision in Philadelphia: The Constitutional Convention of 1787 (coauthored with

Christopher Collier). New York, NY: Random House, 1986.

Duke Ellington. New York, NY: Oxford University Press, 1987.

Duke Ellington. New York, NY: Macmillan, 1991.

The Empty Mirror. New York, NY: Bloomsbury, 2004.

Give Dad My Best. Bristol, FL: Four Winds, 1976.

The Great Jazz Artists. Bristol, FL: Four Winds, 1977.

Inside Jazz. Bristol, FL: Four Winds, 1973.

It's Murder at St. Basket's. New York, NY: Grosset, 1972.

Jazz: An American Saga. New York, NY: Holt, 1997.

The Jazz Kid. New York, NY: Holt, 1994.

Jump Ship to Freedom (coauthored with Christopher Collier). New York, NY: Delacorte, 1981.

Louis Armstrong: An American Success Story. New York, NY: Macmillan, 1985.

Making Music for Money. New York, NY: Franklin Watts, 1976.

The Making of Jazz: A Comprehensive History. Boston, MA: Houghton Mifflin, 1978.

Me and Billy. New York, NY: Marshall Cavendish, 2004.

My Brother Sam Is Dead (coauthored with Christopher Collier). Bristol, FL: Four Winds, 1974.

My Crooked Family. New York, NY: Simon & Schuster, 1991.

Outside Looking In. New York, NY: Macmillan, 1987.

Practical Music Theory: How Music Is Put Together from Bach to Rock. New York, NY: W. W. Norton, 1970.

Rich and Famous: The Further Adventures of George Stable. Bristol, FL: Four Winds, 1975.

Rock Star. Bristol, FL: Four Winds, 1970.

The Teddy Bear Habit; or, How I Became a Winner. New York, NY: W. W. Norton, 1967.

A Visit to the Fire House. New York, NY: W. W. Norton, 1967.

War Comes to Willy Freeman (coauthored with Christopher Collier). New York, NY: Delacorte, 1983.

When the Stars Begin to Fall. New York, NY: Delacorte, 1986.

Which Musical Instrument Shall I Play? New York, NY: W. W. Norton, 1969.

Who Is Carrie? (coauthored with Christopher Collier). New York, NY: Delacorte, 1984.

Wild Boy. New York, NY: Marshall Cavendish, 2002.

The Winchesters. New York, NY: Macmillan, 1988.

The Winter Hero (coauthored with Christopher Collier). Bristol, FL: Four Winds, 1978.

With Every Drop of Blood (coauthored with
    Christopher Collier). New York, NY:
    Delacorte, 1994.
*The Worst of Times: A Story of the Great
    Depression.* Lincolnwood, IL: Jamestown
    Publishers, 2000.

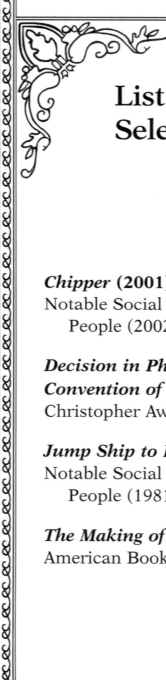

List of
Selected Awards

***Chipper* (2001)**
Notable Social Studies Trade Book for Young
   People (2002)

***Decision in Philadelphia: The Constitutional
Convention of 1787* (1987)**
Christopher Award (1987)

***Jump Ship to Freedom* (1981)**
Notable Social Studies Trade Book for Young
   People (1981)

***The Making of Jazz* (1978)**
American Book Award Finalist (1978)

My Brother Sam Is Dead **(1974)**

American Library Association (ALA) Notable
   Book (1975)
Jane Addams Honor Book Award (1975)
National Book Award Finalist (1975)
Newbery Honor Book (1975)
Phoenix Award (1994)

Rock Star **(1970)**

Child Study Children's Book Committee Best
   Books of the Year (1970)

War Comes to Willy Freeman **(1983)**

Notable Social Studies Trade Books for Young
   People (1983)

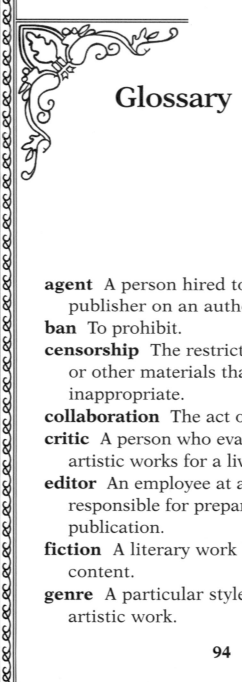

Glossary

agent A person hired to negotiate with a publisher on an author's behalf.

ban To prohibit.

censorship The restriction of access to books or other materials that are considered inappropriate.

collaboration The act of working together.

critic A person who evaluates literary and artistic works for a living.

editor An employee at a publishing house responsible for preparing a manuscript for publication.

fiction A literary work based on imagined content.

genre A particular style of literary or artistic work.

historical novel A work of book-length fiction that deals with historic events.

irony The use of words to suggest the opposite of their literal meaning.

manuscript A typed or handwritten copy of a book submitted by an author for publication.

narrator The character in a book that tells the story.

nonfiction A literary work based on factual content.

pacifist A person against war or violence.

profanity Offensive or vulgar words.

prolific Producing many works or results.

protagonist The main character in a literary work.

saga A long, sometimes multipart narrative.

sequel A literary work that continues the story in another previously written work.

setting The location and time period in which a story takes place.

trilogy A group of three literary works on the same subject.

For More Information

Web Sites

Due to the changing nature of Internet links, the Rosen Publishing Group, Inc., has developed an online list of Web sites related to the subject of this book. This site is updated regularly. Please use this link to access the list:

http://www.rosenlinks.com/lab/jalc

For Further Reading

Collier, Christopher. *Brother Sam and All That.* Orange, CT: Clearwater Press, 1999.

Foerstel, Herbert N. *Banned in the U.S.A.: A Reference Guide to Book Censorship in Schools and Public Libraries.* Rev. ed. Westport, CT: Greenwood Press, 2002.

Gallo, Donald R., ed. *Speaking for Ourselves: Autobiographical Sketches by Notable Authors of Books for Young Adults.* Urbana, IL: National Council of Teachers of English, 1990.

McCarthy, Tara. *Scholastic Literature Guide: My Brother Is Dead.* New York, NY: Scholastic, 1997.

McElmeel, Sharron L. "Christopher Collier and James Lincoln Collier." *Book Report*, Vol. 15, September/October 1996, pp. 28–30.

Bibliography

American Library Association. "Challenged and Banned Books." Retrieved May 15, 2004 (http://www.ala.org/ala/oif/bannedbooksweek/challengedbanned/challengedbanned.htm).

American Library Association. "Reporting a Challenge." Retrieved June 5, 2004 (http://www.ala.org/ala/oif/challengesupport/reporting/reportingchallenge.htm).

Children's Literature Review. Vol. 3. Detroit, MI: Gale Research, 1979.

"Christopher and James Lincoln Collier." *St. James Guide to Young Adult Writers*. 2nd ed. New York, NY: St. James Press, 1999. Reproduced in Biography Resource Center. Farmington Hills, MI: The Gale

Group, 2004. Retrieved May 15, 2004 (http://galenet.galegroup.com/servlet/BioRC).

Collier, Christopher. *Brother Sam and All That*. Orange, CT: Clearwater Press, 1999.

Collier, Christopher. "Fact, Fiction and History: The Role of Historian, Writer, Teacher and Reader." *ALAN Review*, Vol. 14, Winter 1987, pp. 7–10.

Collier, Christopher. "Johnny and Sam: Old and New Approaches to the American Revolution." *Horn Book Magazine*, Vol. 52, April 1976, pp. 132–138.

Collier, James Lincoln. Autobiographical sketch. *Fifth Book of Junior Authors*. New York, NY: H. W. Wilson, 1983. Retrieved May 15, 2004 (http://www.edupaperback.org/showauth.cfm?authid=49).

Collier, James Lincoln. "Doing the Literary Tango." *ALAN Review*, Vol. 14, Winter 1987, pp. 4–5.

"Eric Johnson, President/CEO Baldwin Ice Cream, Forces School District in Chicago Suburb to Remove Book Containing Racial Slurs." *Jet*, Vol. 91, December 2, 1996, pp. 23–24.

Foerstel, Herbert N. *Banned in the U.S.A.: A Reference Guide to Book Censorship in Schools and Public Libraries*. Rev. ed. Westport, CT: Greenwood Press, 2002.

Gallo, Donald R., ed. *Speaking for Ourselves: Autobiographical Sketches by Notable Authors of Books for Young Adults*. Urbana, IL: National Council of Teachers of English, 1990.

"James Lincoln Collier." *Authors and Artists for Young Adults*. Vol. 13. Detroit, MI: Gale Research, 1994. Reproduced in Biography Resource Center. Farmington Hills, MI: The Gale Group, 2004. Retrieved May 15, 2004 (http://galenet.galegroup.com/servlet/BioRC).

"James Lincoln Collier." Contemporary Authors Online. Gale, 2004. Reproduced in Biography Resource Center. Farmington Hills, MI: The Gale Group, 2004. Retrieved May 15, 2004 (http://galenet.galegroup.com/servlet/BioRC).

Kovacs, Deborah. *Meet the Authors: 25 Writers of Upper Elementary and Middle School Books Talk About Their Work*. New York, NY: Scholastic Professional Books, 1995.

Kristl, Carol. "Virginia School to Keep Novel About Black Slave on Shelf." *American Libraries*, Vol. 24, July/August 1993, p. 602.

McCarthy, Tara. *Scholastic Literature Guide: My Brother Sam Is Dead*. New York, NY: Scholastic, 1997.

McElmeel, Sharron L. "Christopher Collier and James Lincoln Collier." *Book Report*, Vol. 15, September/October 1996, pp. 28–30.

McElmeel, Sharron L. *100 Most Popular Children's Authors: Biographical Sketches and Bibliographies*. Englewood, CO: Libraries Unlimited, 1999.

Random House. "Author Spotlight: James Collier." Retrieved May 12, 2004 (http://www.randomhouse.com/teens/authors/results.pperl?authorid=5394).

Source Notes

Chapter 1

1. James Lincoln Collier, "Doing the Literary Tango," *ALAN Review*, Vol. 14, Winter 1987, pp. 4–5.
2. Deborah Kovacs, *Meet the Authors: 25 Writers of Upper Elementary and Middle School Books Talk About Their Work* (New York, NY: Scholastic Professional Books, 1995), p. 15.
3. Ibid.
4. Ibid.
5. James Lincoln Collier, Autobiographical sketch, *Fifth Book of Junior Authors* (New York, NY: H. W. Wilson, 1983). Retrieved May 15, 2004 (http://www.edupaperback.org/showauth.cfm?authid=49).
6. Kovacs, p. 14.
7. Donald R. Gallo, ed. *Speaking for Ourselves: Autobiographical Sketches by Notable Authors*

of Books for Young Adults (Urbana, IL: National
Council of Teachers of English, 1990), p. 46.
8. Ibid.
9. James Lincoln Collier, Autobiographical sketch.
10. *Children's Literature Review*, Vol. 3 (Detroit, MI:
Gale Research, 1979), p. 44.
11. Ibid., p. 49.
12. "James Lincoln Collier," *Authors and Artists for
Young Adults*, Vol. 13 (Detroit, MI: Gale Research,
1994). Reproduced in Biography Resource Center
(Farmington Hills, MI: The Gale Group, 2004).
Retrieved May 15, 2004 (http://galenet.galegroup.
com/servlet/BioRC).

Chapter 2
1. "James Lincoln Collier," *Authors and Artists for
Young Adults*, Vol. 13 (Detroit, MI: Gale Research,
1994). Reproduced in Biography Resource Center
(Farmington Hills, MI: The Gale Group, 2004).
Retrieved May 15, 2004 (http://galenet.galegroup.
com/servlet/BioRC).
2. Donald R. Gallo, ed. *Speaking for Ourselves:
Autobiographical Sketches by Notable Authors of
Books for Young Adults* (Urbana, IL: National
Council of Teachers of English, 1990), p. 44.
3. Sharron L. McElmeel, "Christopher Collier and
James Lincoln Collier," *Book Report*, Vol. 15,
September/October 1996, p. 28.
4. "James Lincoln Collier," Contemporary Authors
Online (Farmington Hills, MI: The Gale Group,

2004). Reproduced in Biography Resource Center (Farmington Hills, MI: The Gale Group, 2004). Retrieved May 15, 2004 (http://galenet.galegroup. com/servlet/BioRC).

5. James Lincoln Collier, "Doing the Literary Tango," *ALAN Review*, Vol. 14, Winter 1987, p. 4.
6. Ibid., p. 5.
7. "James Lincoln Collier," Contemporary Authors Online.
8. Sharron L. McElmeel, *100 Most Popular Children's Authors: Biographical Sketches and Bibliographies* (Englewood, CO: Libraries Unlimited, 1999), p. 87.
9. James Lincoln Collier, "Doing the Literary Tango," p. 4.

Chapter 3

1. "James Lincoln Collier," *Authors and Artists for Young Adults*, Vol. 13 (Detroit, MI: Gale Research, 1994). Reproduced in Biography Resource Center (Farmington Hills, MI: The Gale Group, 2004). Retrieved May 15, 2004 (http://galenet.galegroup. com/servlet/BioRC).
2. Ibid.
3. James Lincoln Collier and Christopher Collier, *My Brother Sam Is Dead* (Bristol, FL: Four Winds, 1974), p. 24.
4. Ibid.
5. Ibid., p. 65.
6. Ibid., p. 167.
7. Ibid., p. 162.

8. Christopher Collier, *Brother Sam and All That* (Orange, CT: Clearwater Press, 1999), p. 39.

9. James Lincoln Collier and Christopher Collier, *My Brother Sam Is Dead*, p. 245.

10. Ibid.

11. James Lincoln Collier and Christopher Collier, *The Bloody Country* (Bristol, FL: Four Winds, 1976), p. 43.

12. Ibid., p. 67.

13. Ibid., p. 181.

14. *Children's Literature Review*, Vol. 3 (Detroit, MI: Gale Research, 1979), p. 44.

15. "James Lincoln Collier," *Authors and Artists for Young Adults*.

16. James Lincoln Collier, "Doing the Literary Tango," *ALAN Review*, Vol. 14, Winter 1987, p. 4.

17. James Lincoln Collier and Christopher Collier, *The Winter Hero* (Bristol, FL: Four Winds, 1978), p. 8.

18. Ibid., p. 64.

19. Ibid., p. 93.

20. Ibid., p. 149.

21. Christopher Collier, *Brother Sam and All That*, p. 111.

22. James Lincoln Collier and Christopher Collier, *The Winter Hero*, pp. 149–150.

Chapter 4

1. James Lincoln Collier and Christopher Collier, *War Comes to Willy Freeman* (New York, NY: Delacorte, 1983), pp. 64–65.

2. Ibid., pp. 63–64.
3. Ibid., p. 172.
4. James Lincoln Collier and Christopher Collier, *Jump Ship to Freedom* (New York, NY: Delacorte, 1983), p. 187.
5. Ibid., p. 111.
6. "James Lincoln Collier," *Authors and Artists for Young Adults*, Vol. 13 (Detroit, MI: Gale Research, 1994). Reproduced in Biography Resource Center (Farmington Hills, MI: The Gale Group, 2004). Retrieved May 15, 2004 (http://galenet.galegroup.com/servlet/BioRC).
7. James Lincoln Collier and Christopher Collier, *Who Is Carrie?* (New York, NY: Delacorte, 1984), p. 11.
8. Ibid., p. 39.
9. Ibid., p. 147.

Chapter 5

1. American Library Association, "Reporting a Challenge." Retrieved June 5, 2004 (http://www.ala.org/ala/oif/challengesupport/reporting/reportingchallenge.htm).
2. Herbert N. Foerstel, *Banned in the U.S.A.: A Reference Guide to Book Censorship in Schools and Public Libraries*, rev. ed. (Westport, CT: Greenwood Press, 2002), p. 209.
3. Ibid., p. 210.
4. Christopher Collier, *Brother Sam and All That* (Orange, CT: Clearwater Press, 1999), pp. 218–219.

5. James Lincoln Collier and Christopher Collier, *My Brother Sam Is Dead* (Bristol, FL: Four Winds, 1974), p. 242.

6. Foerstel, p. 210.

7. Ibid., p. 55.

8. Christopher Collier, "Johnny and Sam: Old and New Approaches to the American Revolution," *Horn Book Magazine*, Vol. 52, April 1976, p. 135.

9. Christopher Collier, *Brother Sam and All That*, p. 229.

10. James Lincoln Collier and Christopher Collier, *Jump Ship to Freedom* (New York, NY: Delacorte, 1983), p. 4–5.

11. Carol Kristl. "Virginia School to Keep Novel About Black Slave on Shelf." *American Libraries*, Vol. 24, July/August 1993, p. 602.

12. James Lincoln Collier and Christopher Collier, *War Comes to Willy Freeman* (New York, NY: Delacorte, 1983), p. 96.

13. Christopher Collier, *Brother Sam and All That*, p. 231.

Chapter 6

1. James Lincoln Collier and Christopher Collier, *The Clock* (New York, NY: Delacorte, 1992), p. 115.

2. "James Lincoln Collier," Contemporary Authors Online (Farmington Hills, MI: The Gale Group, 2004). Reproduced in Biography Resource Center (Farmington Hills, MI: The Gale Group, 2004).

Retrieved May 15, 2004 (http://galenet.galegroup.
com/servlet/BioRC).

3. Random House, "Author Spotlight: James Collier."
Retrieved May 12, 2004 (http://www.randomhouse.
com/teens/authors/results.pperl?authorid=5394).

Chapter 7

1. "James Lincoln Collier," *Authors and Artists for
Young Adults*, Vol. 13 (Detroit, MI: Gale Research,
1994). Reproduced in Biography Resource Center
(Farmington Hills, MI: The Gale Group, 2004).
Retrieved May 15, 2004
(http://galenet.galegroup.com/servlet/BioRC).

2. James Lincoln Collier, *Making Music for Money*
(New York, NY: Franklin Watts, 1976), p. 25.

3. *Children's Literature Review*, Vol. 3 (Detroit, MI:
Gale Research, 1979), p. 46.

4. Ibid.

5. James Lincoln Collier, *The Jazz Kid* (New York,
NY: Henry Holt, 1994), p. 25.

6. Donald R. Gallo, ed. *Speaking for Ourselves:
Autobiographical Sketches by Notable Authors of
Books for Young Adults*. (Urbana, IL: National
Council of Teachers of English, 1990), p. 47.

7. Ibid.

Index

About the Author

Liz Sonneborn is a writer and an editor living in Brooklyn, New York. A graduate of Swarthmore College, she has written more than thirty books for children and adults, including *The American West*, *A to Z of American Women in the Performing Arts*, and *The New York Public Library's Amazing Native American History*, winner of a 2000 Parent's Choice Award. As a child, James Lincoln Collier's *The Teddy Bear Habit* was her favorite book.

Photo Credits

Courtesy James Lincoln Collier

Designer: Tahara Anderson
Editor: Christine Poolos
Photo Researcher: Hillary Arnold